MOTTOES FOR MANAGING

MOTTOES FOR MANAGING

J. ROBERT PARKINSON

PELICAN PUBLISHING COMPANY
Gretna 2006

---

*The word "Pelican" and the depiction of a pelican are
trademarks of Pelican Publishing Company, Inc., and
are registered in the U.S. Patent and Trademark Office.*

Library of Congress Cataloging-in-Publication Data

Parkinson, J. Robert (John Robert)
    Mottoes for managing / J. Robert Parkinson.
        p. cm.
    ISBN-13: 978-1-58980-402-9 (pbk. : alk. paper)
    1. Management.   2. Management--Quotations, maxims, etc.
I. Title.
    HD31.P297 2006
    658--dc22

                                                    2006012363

Printed in the United States of America

Published by Pelican Publishing Company, Inc.
1000 Burmaster Street, Gretna, Louisiana 70053

To my wife, Eileen, always a great inspiration

I recently published a book I wrote with a coauthor in which we set out a series of specific steps and techniques necessary to become a successful manager. We worked hard to keep the text short and uncomplicated, and I believe we succeeded. When I reread the book I realized it would be possible—and helpful—to focus even more economically on words and to use a wide range of brief ideas to spark additional thoughts about the important tasks of managing and communicating.

I hope the adages, proverbs, and mottoes I've selected and related to managing and communicating will encourage you to see these lines in a new light. Using such lines in daily activity might help all of us view our jobs and responsibilities with a fresh and challenging perspective.

Taking a few seconds to read these short, memorable quotations could result in deeper and extended thoughts about managing others.

From the time we were little children such short "sayings" have helped us learn important basics to use as adults.

Remember these lines?

"Early to bed, early to rise makes a person healthy, wealthy, and wise."

"A stitch in time saves nine."

"As you sow, so shall you reap."

Even today, when we encounter these short sentences they trigger ideas far larger and far more complex than their brevity would suggest.

Often, when we look at something from a different point of view it takes on totally new dimensions.

I hope the lines I have selected and the thoughts I have shared will touch some nerves and entice you to consider how this free association can help you become a better manager and communicator.

Finally, I'd like to hear from you—and learn about two items:
First, your reactions to my selections. Second, your suggestions
of other lines and anecdotes all of us might use.

Enjoy.

MOTTOES FOR MANAGING

There are those that look
at things the way they are,
and ask why?
I dream of things
that never were,
and ask why not?

Robert Kennedy

This quotation is all about attitude! The degree of success each of us achieves in our business and personal lives is affected by what we believe. Our beliefs drive our actions, and those actions always have consequences.

Here is a new set of "ABCs" to remember: Attitudes, Behaviors, Consequences. And they can be as important as the ones we all learned years ago in school.

Although there are always some factors we can't control, there are also many we can control. Here's an example.

A physician friend of mine took charge of his own health in the best way he could to prevent serious consequences. He was motivated because both his father and his older brother had died of heart attacks when they were in their mid-forties. He didn't want that to happen to him.

He exercised, dieted, and did everything he could to stay healthy.

However, at the age of forty-four he had a heart attack. Just like his father and brother. But he survived.

He told me, "I controlled everything I could to maintain good health. The one thing I couldn't control was the genes I had inherited. But, if I hadn't done everything else, I too would have died."

"It would have been easy," he said, "to just accept what I knew was inevitable. I was going to have heart trouble, but why not fight it in every way I could?"

He fought; and he won. He is now sixty-two.

His attitude led to his behavior; and his behavior led to the exact consequences he wanted.

Think about this principle in your business life. Don't simply accept what you think might be inevitable. Take action and influence the outcome.

Don't ask, "Why"; ask "Why not?"

Then do it!

He who can, does.
He who cannot, teaches.

George Bernard Shaw

Like other mottoes, this one too is all about attitude. But it often reflects academic behavior.

Although it is often spoken or written as a derogatory comment, or as a "put down," I suggest you consider it another way.

Entirely different skills and talents are necessary for performing and for instructing. Talented teachers often produce students who are more talented and more capable than the teachers.

It's the teachers' talent, ability, and commitment that guide and encourage their students to higher levels of achievement.

In every business there are teachers, and there are students. The teachers, of course, are the managers; and the students are the members of the staff.

An important role of a good manager is to be a teacher. It is the manager's responsibility to get others to perform—not to do the work himself. If a manager does the work, he is a doer—not a manager.

I once offered a series of seminars on this topic. It was titled, "Getting Work Done Through People," and that title is right on target as a descriptor.

The skills and talents needed to manage and to teach are very different from those needed to follow directions and perform.

Don't look at this motto as a description and comparison of ability, but rather as a separation and designation of ability.

Someone who "does" is not better than someone who "teaches"—or vice versa. Each has his specific responsibilities. If those responsibilities are carried out to the best of the individual's ability, they complement each other, and they contribute to the success of the organization.

We miss you most
 when you're home.
                    Seven-year-old son of a friend

A few years ago, I was working with a group of young, successful executives. At one of our regular meetings the discussion turned to family responsibilities and the pressures of business travel. Everyone agreed that travel was difficult but necessary. It was an important part of their success.

One of the men, Steve, brought us all up short and changed the course of the discussion with this story.

He had returned home from an "important" business trip one Friday evening and spent most of the day Saturday doing the paperwork required to close out the trip. On Sunday he began packing his suitcase and briefcase when his seven-year-old son asked him to play catch with him in the backyard.

Steve explained he couldn't play because he "had" to get ready for the upcoming trip. Seeing that the little boy was disappointed, Steve said to him, "Tommy, you know I have to take these trips even though I don't want to. I miss you and Mom so much when I'm away."

Tommy knew there would be no game of catch—again. His father was too busy. With a tear in his eye, Tommy said, "I know you miss us, Dad; and we miss you too when you're away.

"But we miss you most when you're home."

Think about that statement for a few minutes, and think about how you affect the most important people in your life.

**Eventually—
why not now?**

Many years ago I saw this sentence presented as a banner news-paper headline. The newspaper was one of those fake papers people can have made up at an amusement park. Usually they are jokes and are intended to be gifts.

I'm not sure whether this one was intended as a joke or not because it was in the office of a building janitor who didn't like to work very much. Everything he did was put off as long as he could get away with it. It certainly was a message about him, but I don't know who gave it to him.

Regardless of the reason, however, it struck me as great wisdom in just four words.

In every job we have during our careers there are tasks we know we have to carry out, but we put them off as long as we can. We all know what they are: performance reviews, report writing, etc. We also know they have to be done—we just don't want to do them.

But they don't go away. They sit on our desks and in our "to do" files and wait for us. The passage of time doesn't make them any eas-ier; in fact we often worry about them to the extent we magnify them out of proportion. Then, when we do them, we often just want to get through with them as quickly as possible and move on to something else. The tasks don't get the attention they deserve.

So, take this old fake newspaper headline to heart when you face an unpleasant task. You have to do it sooner or later, so why not right away? Get it "off your plate" by taking control of the situation.

Gather your thoughts and your resources and face the task with this positive attitude: "This task is a necessary part of my job so I'll do it well, and I'll do it *now.*"

It works!

**If anything is worth doing,
it is worth doing well.**

In order to complete any job or assignment, you must devote time, talent, energy, and resources. Nothing happens all by itself. Some kind of work is necessary.

Since that's the case—you're going to have to perform some task, and it just makes sense to do it right the first time. The other way to look at it, of course, is this way: If something isn't worth doing—don't do it! Don't waste the time, the talent, the energy, or the resources. Just don't bother. You would just be spinning your wheels.

If, on the other hand, you determine the task must be undertaken and completed, you might just as well focus on performing quality service rather than simply filling up time. And time is a nonrenewable commodity. Once it's used, once it has passed, that's it! You can't go back and recapture it. It's gone.

Every one of us is evaluated on performance, and that evaluation includes not only accomplishing tasks, but also doing so within the allocated time frame.

Since every job requires "spending time on task," it just makes sense to use that time as well as we can.

**Don't confuse the
immediate
with the
important.**

It's easy to get caught up in details rather than to focus on issues.

I worked with a man who was a "list-maker," and he was convinced it was the best way for him to carry out his job responsibilities. He wrote his lists on three-by-five index cards, which he kept in his shirt pocket. This was long before electronic pocket computer devices. His intentions were good since he planned to "cross off" each task when it was completed.

He wrote everything that was important for him to accomplish. However, almost without exception, at the end of his very busy days most of the items remained on the index cards. He worked long and hard, but most of what he did during the day fell into the category of "reacting."

He solved problems, responded to emergencies, jumped quickly to avoid crises, and kept his personal ship on course by responding to changing conditions. His days were full, and he was tired at the end of each workday, but the list remained intact. He didn't accomplish what he intended to because he lost sight of his goals. Each successive day had a list almost identical to that of the previous day.

Certainly, there is a need to react and respond and to jump in many work-related positions, but you should never lose sight of what you desire. You must know where you want to go in order to set a course.

Reaching a goal is the "important"; reacting to obstacles is the "immediate."

Be sure you know which is which in both your personal and professional life.

Listen more
than you *talk.*

There is a rather silly saying about listening and talking. It says, "If we were supposed to talk more than listen, we would have two mouths and one ear, but that's not how we're built." The number of organs shouldn't be the determiner. The determiner should be a mind-set.

The world outside each of us has been around for a long time, and it is populated by a great many creatures. We are a single being, and we're here for a relatively short time.

We can have an impact and leave a mark on the world if we use our talents well. In our business relationships we work to influence others to buy, to support, to allow, to participate, or to take some other kind of action.

The best way to accomplish those tasks is to learn about others. They know themselves and what is important to them before we make any suggestions, recommendations, offers, or pleas to them.

We learn by taking in information, and listening is one of the best ways to do that. When we are talking, information is going out but not coming in. Certainly there is a time for talking, but we are more effective when we have good data to talk about.

The same argument can be made about having two eyes, of course, but the point is obvious.

Input must precede output if the output is to be of any value.

**It is easier to get forgiveness
than permission.**

When I first heard this comment, my reaction was to think it was backwards. I thought if I asked for permission, it would keep me safe. I wouldn't make any mistakes or move into any areas where I didn't belong. Also, I would avoid the need to ask for forgiveness because I wouldn't do anything wrong in the first place. It seemed that asking for permission was a way to stay out of trouble.

That seemed to make good sense.

However, I learned that playing-it-safe behavior often got in the way of making progress, or being able to show what I could do. Here's why.

If I asked for permission to do something, my supervisor often did one of two things. Either he said he was too busy to discuss the matter at the moment, or he asked question after question to attempt to learn as much as possible about the action I was proposing. Both courses consumed a great deal of time, and all too often a fair decision was delayed. From my supervisor's perspective it was easier and safer to say no to my request. As a result, little was accomplished.

When I discovered that fact and felt comfortable with the notion of making decisions, I realized that most of the time my decisions and recommendations would be good and of value to the company. My taking the initiative was always appreciated by my boss, because it made him look good too. When I did make a bad decision, though, it was identified and corrected. That also made my boss look good.

The strength lay in the fact that action was taken without asking for permission. The company prospered. I knew not to do anything foolish or irresponsible, because I was aware of the goals of the company.

A good boss will respect initiative and decision making when it promotes company goals.

Asking for permission can slow down a project because too many people must participate in the decision. When you make decisions, projects move ahead. If some corrections are necessary along the line, that's okay because you are still moving. That's dynamic.

Waiting for someone else to make a decision is static. Taking the initiative is active.

Say what you mean,
and
mean what you say.

Sister Mary Rosita

I remember this lesson from the first grade in grammar school. Sister Mary Rosita must have made a strong impression on me because it's been a long time since I've been in the first grade. But it was excellent advice then, and it continues to be great advice today.

In all of our business communication, internal, external, to superiors or subordinates, we must be clear about our messages before we deliver them. We must also be aware that those messages are not only the words we use but also how we say them and how we look when we're saying them.

The lyrics of an old song sum up this fact in just a few words, "It ain't what you say, it's the way that you say it."

Here is another caution. The true message isn't what you intend to say, but what the receiver thinks you mean. It's not what you say; it's what the receiver thinks you are saying.

Before you deliver any message to any employee or staff member, think first about how that person is going to interpret what you deliver. Select the time, place, and conditions that will support your thoughts and assure clear understanding of your message. That way you will say what you mean and not just what you feel.

Then be sure to back up your thoughts and words by standing behind them. That subsequent performance will not only support your words but will add strength to all of your subsequent communication.

Words alone without action will become hollow. They will not be listened to with any intensity.

If you deliver that kind of message to any of your employees, your effectiveness will be severely diminished.

Sister Mary Rosita was on to something years ago.

Listen to her today.

**Whatever you do—
do it on purpose!**

J. Robert Parkinson

Most of our daily lives are filled with activities and actions that we carry out by habit. These activities and actions include writing, talking, walking, etc., most of which don't require any particular thought on our part. We just do them, and we do them because they are comfortable to us. That's what habits are, and why they're so easy to form and follow. They are behaviors that don't require any thought, and they feel good.

Because they feel good, we continue to do them; and because we continue to do them, they continue to feel good. There is a clear cycle here, and it will continue until there is some good reason to change.

In dealing with our employees and staff members we often act out of habit too. If something seemed to work well yesterday, last week, last month, or last year, we keep on doing it. The problem is this: What worked well in the past with a specific group of people might not work as well now and in the future with other groups of people. What we intend a message to mean, for example, might not be understood that way by the people to whom we are sending the message.

So make a conscious decision to speak and act in ways that will be significant and will be understood by those you are addressing.

Don't simply say and do things that *feel* good. Say and do things that *are* good!

If you consider the people, the conditions, and the timing before you speak and act, you'll discover something interesting. Your communication will be more effective because you will be tailoring your messages to fit the individual rather than assuming that "one size fits all."

Don't make the individual work to fit the message. Work to make the message fit the individual.

**Build bridges—
not walls.**

Many years ago a friend told me a story—no, a fable—which has a strong message for everyday business and personal relationships.

Two little ants lived near a small stream. There were many grains of sand nearby, and being busy little ants, they worked on moving those grains of sand from one place to another to clear the land and make their lives safer and more comfortable.

One of the ants piled up the sand so it made a long, high wall. "That will keep out all the other ants so I won't have to worry about them getting too close to me," he said.

The other ant moved the grains of sand so they went all across the small stream. He had made a little bridge. "That will help me get around just in case something changes around here," he said.

One day it rained so hard the land flooded. The ant that had built the wall couldn't get away because the wall was in the way. His wall trapped him in a place he thought would be safe.

The other ant ran across the bridge he had built and went up to higher ground. He was safe because the bridge he had built gave him a choice of where he could be.

That little story from my friend brought home this simple truth: If we build bridges, we can adjust to changing conditions. If we build walls, we limit our options.

In business, if we reach out and use all the tools available to us, we build relationships and associations that will allow us to change and grow under changing conditions. If we lock ourselves in and limit our contacts and opportunities, we may very well be trapped by our own actions.

Bridges allow us to move, to explore, to grow. Walls keep us confined, restricted, and isolated.

As the business world continues to change, it's easy to figure out what we should build—bridges, not walls.

By med'cine
life may be prolonged,
yet death Will seize
the doctor too.

Shakespeare
Cymbeline

I have a colleague who has a plaque on his desk that provokes a wide variety of reactions from visitors to his office. The plaque states:

"In one hundred years—all new people."

Some visitors laugh; some are taken aback; and some are shocked.

He sees it as a philosophy and as a reminder to do the best he can in every aspect of his personal and business lives.

In his words, "Many have gone before us, and they have provided a legacy for us. Now it's our turn. We must be good stewards of what we have inherited, and we must pass on the best we can to those who come after us."

He describes the need to concentrate on and foster certain "core values" in every aspect of his life.

Just as the doctor, by his talents and his tools, prolongs life by years and decades, in time someone else will replace him. Perhaps it will be another doctor with the same specialty, and then in time, he too will be replaced.

This saying isn't morbid. Rather it should be seen as inspirational and challenging.

When we consider all those "new" people, we should be encouraged and motivated to perform at our best right now—to continue and to pass on the "core values" that define our lives and our businesses.

Yes, in time there will be "all new people," but that focus is exciting and challenging. It can encourage us to achieve new heights.

We all have strength enough
to endure
the misfortunes
of others.

La Rochefoucauld
"Maxim 19"

How many times have we heard others (and sometimes ourselves), say something like, "You'll get over this," or, "Just keep a stiff upper lip."

Most of us have been in positions where we have dispensed that kind of advice, and it can be pretty shallow and unwelcome.

When misfortunes befall others, all we observe is surface information. We have no idea of the feelings, the repercussions, and the emotional impact on the affected parties. We are quick to offer a hollow comment like, "I know how you feel." But we don't know! So we shouldn't say it!

The workplace is filled with real live unique people, not with interchangeable mechanical employees. As a manager you have to keep that fact in mind all the time. You are dealing with people who have wants, needs, feelings, desires, and fears. You are not working with beings who simply have a job to do or a task to perform for eight hours a day.

Get to know the people you work with so you don't talk in platitudes and offer simplistic solutions to what you think their problems might be.

Work to know the person behind the employee.

**Usually
we praise
only
to be praised.**

**La Rochefoucauld
"Maxim 146"**

When the motivation for giving praise is to receive praise in return, it is shallow and selfish. The praise is suspect, and any positive consequences will be short lived.

Many managers are guilty of such shallow praise and hollow words. They think that if they praise others—or at least don't correct them—they will be seen as "good guys." They think their staff will like them. Feelings based on that philosophy don't last long.

I know a manager who worked very hard to be "praised" by those who reported to him. In face-to-face conversations he was always complimentary and strove to be popular and well-liked.

The problems came after the face-to-face conversations. He didn't back up and demonstrate his words in other settings with other participants.

This failure resulted in his staff seeing him as hypocritical. He didn't intend to project such a negative image, but that's exactly what he did. Now, his managing days are declining.

Praise must be honest, and it must be consistent. That way, when correction is necessary, it will be seen in context. It won't be criticism; it will be guidance.

Managers work with many personalities, and that's tough. Consistency provides managers with excellent navigation tools, and the managers' "North Star" will always be simply doing the right thing.

Give praise not to get it returned, but because it is the right thing to do!

A journey of a
thousand miles
begins
with a single step.

Chinese proverb

This line has been used for so long by so many people that it seems trite. The suggestion is so simple it's a wonder why so many people don't follow it.

Just start! That's all there is to it.

Time is a nonrenewable commodity, and if it isn't used well today it's gone. There is no way to save it to be used another day. So use it when you have it.

Many of the tasks that face us in our business lives can seem large and daunting. So much so that we are intimidated by what might be required of us. And all too often that intimidation results in inaction. We never start! The failure to begin guarantees we'll never finish.

I have a close friend who has a great idea for a book, and from everything I know about him, he'll be able to write it, and write it well.

But there's a big problem. He hasn't started writing it, even though he's been talking about wanting to write it for more than three years. Those past three years can't ever be recaptured, but I'm still hoping he'll begin writing the book—someday—soon.

Look around at your business, social, and family lives, and identify some things you always wanted to do: Things that are big, far away, perhaps intimidating.

Pick one, and decide what you want to do about it. Then just take a small step to get started.

That first step is the hardest one, so once you have that one past you, the rest will be a lot easier.

**What goes up
must come down.**

This is an interesting example of generally accepted knowledge. Everybody knows this line, and in the past it seemed to be absolutely true—but not any longer.

Gravity, of course, still exists, but now we all know that if something is sent up high enough, fast enough, and at the correct angle, it will stay up. It will go into orbit! So, a satellite that goes up, stays up—at least for a very long time.

What does this illustration have to do with managing and with business? Simply stated, we should look at things we think are absolutely true and realize they may not be so absolutely true. Times change, conditions change, people change; and we have to look at situations in light of those changes. The world is different from what it was a generation ago. Basic principles and ethics remain, but applications vary.

Knowing about satellites and orbits doesn't negate gravity. On the contrary, understanding gravity, speed, trajectories, etc. is what makes it possible to put a satellite into orbit. It reflects the application of knowledge in new and challenging situations.

Understanding our staff and the pressures of today's business world will assist us to modify and adapt what we think we know to changing conditions.

Adhering to certain behaviors just because "that's the way we've always done it" might not be our best course of action.

Look for ways to adapt and apply what you know from past experiences to new situations.

To thine own self
be true.

Shakespeare
Hamlet

This was excellent advice four centuries ago, and it's still good advice today!

As we interact with a wide variety of people during our business days, we encounter all kinds of pressures, opportunities, demands, and options. Things and people come at us from all directions, and they pull us in all directions too. It's difficult to stay on course. The one true guiding influence in each of us is just that—us.

Each one of us has to look into the mirror every day and face who we are—and we have to live with who we are.

It's often difficult to know how to respond to pressures and opportunities, but consider this thought. Every decision we make becomes a very simple yes-or-no choice.

The most complicated situations and problems we face eventually require us to say either yes or no. Will we do something or not? Sooner or later, decisions about hiring or firing, transferring or promoting, assigning or reassigning, although complicated, all become yes-or-no choices.

As you consider demands, pressures, and options, keep thinking about them until you can say yes or no. If you respond too quickly, you may make choices that are inappropriate; and you'll have to revisit the decision. That's not a good use of your time, and it's a potential problem with your staff relationships.

Elsewhere in this book there is another motto that is appropriate here: "Whatever you do—do it on purpose!"

That one can serve as a good reminder of this one: "To thine own self be true."

Common sense
is not so
common.

                                        Voltaire

How often have we heard people say, "It's just common sense"? If it were common, however, there would probably be far fewer bad decisions made by managers—and by all of us.

A good friend of mine told me a variation of this saying, which I think is an excellent reminder for everyone. One day I said to him that something was common sense, and he said to me, "It may be common sense, but it isn't common practice."

I must admit, every time I'm tempted to describe something as being common sense, I think of my friend's comment, and I pause.

Here is another reason to consider the "common sense" phrase: When someone says to another, "It's just common sense," or some variation of that sentence, it could be taken as a mild insult. It's close to saying that something is so obvious and clear the other person should already know the answer. No one should ever be insulted accidentally by an ill-chosen comment, so we must be aware of that possibility in our daily activity.

Something that makes sense and is sound deserves to be thought of as special and of merit. All of our business relationships deserve clear thought and conscious decisions. If those choices fit generally accepted principles, that's fine. They should be preserved and repeated.

If it makes them "common sense," so be it; and that's a good way to run a business.

We have just enough religion
to make us hate,
but not enough to make us
love one another.

Jonathan Swift

As you consider this motto, expand your thinking beyond the realm of theology. History is filled with examples of the ways people have used religion to harm, persecute, and even kill others in the name of their deity.

But look at this love-hate drive from another, nonreligious perspective. The two sides of this coin lead to very different behaviors.

The "hate" side evokes suspicion, distrust, and jealousy. Managers can create a work environment in which these negative feelings and attitudes drive their own behaviors as well as the behaviors of the people who report to them. "Hate" can result in conformance or obedience, but those behaviors can quickly change when challenged.

On the other hand, the "love" side can produce support, cooperation, and partnership. Those activities are strong and long lasting. They will survive challenges and difficult situations.

As a manager, consider your true motivators. Most managers, in their hearts, want to be successful. Success isn't earned simply by numbers, but by contribution, by growth, and by consistent performance.

Use that positive motivation you have to see the positive contribution your staff members can make. They too want to be successful, and if you demonstrate the support and guidance (the love) they seek, in time they will respond in kind.

The result will be a workplace that is harmonious, supportive, encouraging, and productive.

And that is not a bad environment in any workplace!

It also works at home. Try it!

There is great skill
in knowing how
to conceal one's skill.

La Rochefoucauld
"Maxim 245"

In our book, *Becoming a Successful Manager,* Jack Grossman and I made a point of describing specific skills a manager can and should use when dealing with his staff. These skills are behaviors that good managers employ deliberately. When they do, their employees respond in the desired way.

Such specific behaviors work in all walks of life—in the way managers treat their spouses and children, for example—but our intention was to focus on the business world.

There is a caution here, however. If what managers are doing is obvious, the reactions could be exactly opposite to the desired ones. No one wants to be manipulated, and if behaviors are seen to be aimed at such manipulation, the other party will "turn off." The effort will have been wasted.

In any sport, when players get very good at something after constant practice, the performance looks easy and natural. But, that easy and natural image didn't just happen. It required work and practice. The skill is eventually transparent. Observers can't see precisely all that is being done; they see only the results.

Managing others requires the application of specific skills, but you must be sure the techniques are not obvious. You must practice, practice, practice, so the managing skills become transparent when you use them. This isn't deception or dishonesty: it's a sign of growth and development.

When you practice, the skills will be transparent, but the results will be obvious. And that's what you want!

**Silence
is the best tactic
for him
who distrusts himself.**

**LaRochefoucauld
"Maxim 79"**

I was struck by this maxim because literature is filled with references to silence. "Silence is golden" we were taught from the time we were children. "If you can't say something nice, don't say anything" is another line I remember from my early years, and I'm sure you do too.

In the business world, with all its pressures and problems, it's very easy to react too quickly and to say or do something in an instant that will later take a long time to clarify and correct.

As we all navigate our daily lives, we must be continuously vigilant. We can't let instincts rule judgment and behavior. And that's why this line is so important.

If we're not sure—really sure—of what should be said, the best course of action is to say nothing, to be silent.

Silence doesn't reflect weakness. On the contrary, it is seen as strength. Hesitation doesn't indicate a lack of confidence. Rather it demonstrates caution is being used. It's easy to react quickly, and it may *feel* good to do so. On the other hand, remaining silent while considering a situation and its options will lead to behavior that *is* good.

Simply said, when you're not sure of what you should say or do in a specific situation, give yourself license to be quiet. Don't react until you're ready and prepared.

Your actions then will be sounder and more appropriate than the quick and sometimes hurtful alternatives.

To succeed in the world,
we do everything we can
to appear successful.

La Rochefoucauld
"Maxim 56"

At first glance this maxim might seem to be deceptive and shallow. But, it isn't. It relates to the notion of the self-fulfilling prophecy. We've all heard about that concept, so let me put it in slightly different words that I hope will drive home the significance of this motto.

A colleague of mine puts it this way: "The way you behave depends upon what you tell yourself."

And he uses this example when he conducts seminars for business clients. He says to the participants: "Think of a time you attended a class or a seminar (maybe this one) and going in you told yourself, 'This is going to be a waste of time. I'm not going to learn anything.'

"What was the result? You were right. You didn't learn anything!

"On the other hand, if you tell yourself, 'This is going to be a valuable experience,' you'll probably leave with something useful."

As a manager, focus on the positive as you observe your staff, your challenges, and your opportunities. This practice isn't simplistic or naive. It just makes good sense!

You're going to use a lot of energy completing your various tasks. If you begin by thinking of what you need to do to appear successful, you'll use your talents to head in the right direction.

Obviously, when you go the right way, you'll reach your goal. Think success, and you'll succeed.

Begin at the beginning . . .
and go on till you come to the end:
then stop.

Lewis Carroll
Alice in Wonderland

This wonderful line from *Alice in Wonderland* is a clear set of directions for approaching any task or challenge.

Whatever position we fill in life, we are constantly facing tasks to be accomplished, problems to be solved, and opportunities to be seized. But life is a continuously moving stream of passing time. Everything happens in a sequence. There is cause and effect in everything we experience.

That discipline of sequence and appreciation of time demands that we avoid hasty actions when dealing with other people. We can't and shouldn't assume they are as familiar with or as convinced of the details of a project, for example, as we are. We must be sure to meet colleagues where they are and assist them to get to where we want them to be. This attitude and action requires discipline, clarity of sequence, and a focus on desired outcomes.

So take your time when starting on a new or corrected course of action. Start at the beginning by identifying the goal and the steps necessary to reach it. Work sequentially through each of the steps until you have reached the goal. When you have done so—stop!

All too often managers and others develop an almost obsessive relationship with a project. Once it is finally completed, they won't let go of it and move on to other opportunities. That notion of "moving on" is an imperative in business because none of us can afford to continue performing the same task indefinitely.

When you get to the end of a project or assignment—stop.

The people who get on in this world
are the people who get up and
look for the circumstances they want
and if they can't find them, make them.
George Bernard Shaw

My first conscious observation of this concept came when I was entering the military. A friend of mine, a retired army officer, gave me some advice that I found valuable then and now..

He said, "The first thing you have to do is assess the situation you are handed. Don't act too quickly, but rather develop a good, clear understanding of what you are facing. If you like what you see before you, take action. If you don't like what you see, make the necessary adjustments before taking the action. Get closer, move away, wait for a better time, change direction, get better supplies, move faster, or slow down. Control the situation as best you can."

All of these suggestions, in a very real sense, change the circumstances you face. Although you may not always be able to change all the specific circumstances, you can control how you react to them. When you control your reactions; and you adjust time, distance, speed, etc., you determine what will be the most effective course of action.

As you face your employees or colleagues, be aware of how they might react to such things as disciplinary action, transfers, reassignments, etc. Construct the situation in which you deal with those requirements. If you don't like a certain time line, for example, change it. Don't discuss disciplinary action in the morning if it will create a bigger problem in the afternoon.

This isn't avoiding making decisions. You can't do that and be good at your job. Rather, this is taking charge of situations, and adjusting them as much as you possibly can to achieve your desired results.

**Important principles
may, and must
be, inflexible.**

**Abraham Lincoln
April 11, 1865**

Regardless of how complex a problem or a situation may seem, the ultimate decision we make about it is a simple yes-or-no choice.

A close friend of mine wrestled with a difficult situation a few years ago. He served as an elected member of a governing board. During his term of office a new chief executive officer was going to be hired. Many outstanding candidates expressed interest. Age, gender, and race differences complicated the situation.

It was clear to my friend that Candidate X was preferred by most of the board, but my friend was opposed to that selection. Many interested local groups applied pressure for my friend to support Candidate X "for the sake of unity." Candidate X was certainly going to be chosen. My friend's "no" vote would make no difference in the outcome, but he was convinced the candidate should not be selected. He also knew the difference in their races would affect the public's reaction to his "no" vote.

His choices were clear: Go along with the majority, or vote his conscience.He voted "no."

When he was questioned about why he made his unpopular choice, his answer was a simple one: "It was complicated because of all the diverse issues involved and the expected subsequent reactions. In the end, however, the choice became easy. I looked at myself in the mirror one morning and asked myself, 'Do you really mean yes, or do you mean no?' When my answer was no, my vote was decided."

All the contemplation and the confusion fell by the wayside. His principles were not compromised for the sake of expediency.

As you go through your days and face the difficult decisions that come from managing others, rely on your set of guiding principles.

Being consistent isn't always easy, but adhering to your basic principles will help you through difficult times.

**Delay
is preferable
to error.**

**Thomas Jefferson
In a letter to George Washington
May 16, 1792**

Many years ago I worked with a man who was very quick to react to any situation. He was impatient with anyone who was slow to act. He was the kind of man who was always "jumping in with both feet."

He was in constant motion—making decisions, doing things, and giving orders. One day, he complained that he found himself covering the same ground and wrestling with the same problems over and over again. In his words, "Even when new problems come up, I have to continue to solve the old ones that don't go away. I run out of time, and there's still so much to do."

He was working hard and running fast to solve problems, but often he was solving the wrong problems. He got things "fixed," but they weren't what needed fixing. For whatever reason, he felt it was necessary for him to be in the middle of all activity and controlling everything that came up.

Eventually, after conversations with colleagues, he came to a dramatic, for him, conclusion. He simply hadn't realized that action without a plan has a great possibility of failure. When he came to that conclusion he gave himself the license to slow down.

Instantaneous reaction gave way to conscious decision making. The pace of his daily activity slowed down, but the productivity of his actions increased.

And we'll all agree that positive outcomes are more important, more satisfying, and more lasting than unfocused activity.

**He who thinks himself
wise . . .
is a great fool.**

Voltaire

We all know at least one person who fits this description!

People who think they have "all the answers" quickly demonstrate to all those around them they don't have the answers.

Unfortunately, all too often many of these people seem to end up in some type of management position. Somehow they convince their superiors they are capable of leading. But, they aren't.

Here is one of the easiest ways to identify the "incompetent manager."

Just look for the person who doesn't ask questions. The incompetent manager only tells, never asks.

The reason is simple. In the mind of the incompetent manager, asking a question is an admission of a lack of information. To that manager, asking a question might indicate to others that someone else knows more than the manager does. The incompetent manager cannot—will not—abide that possibility.

Recently, I worked on a consulting project for a company that had such a bad manager heading up a very important part of the organization.

In the three years he was in that position his behavior had succeeded in alienating almost every member of the group he headed. No one—and I mean no one—who reported to him had any respect for him. The universal question among the entire group was, "What does he do to keep his job?" What a question to ask about one's manager!

Everyone wondered about his tenure, but no one wondered about his ability—or his perception of himself.

He thinks he is wise, but you know the rest of the motto.

If you can't write it down,
you probably can't do it.
There is a discipline to
the blank piece of paper.

How many times have we thought we could do something or say something well only to discover we weren't successful when we tried to do so?

I thought a great deal about this situation when I was working with college students who were preparing for job interviews. I would ask them some of the standard Human Resource Department questions like, "What is your greatest strength?" and "What do you want to be doing in five years?"

Even though these aren't the best questions to ask in an interview, it's certain they will be asked by many HR people, so I felt the students should be ready for them. I wanted to see how they would respond. And I wanted them to evaluate their own responses.

Most of them stumbled when asked these questions because they weren't clear about what they wanted to say. In a very real sense they fooled themselves into thinking they could answer the questions, but they discovered they couldn't actually say the words when it counted.

So I had them write down their responses. I didn't expect them to memorize what they wrote, nor did I want them to do so. I did, however, want them to face that blank piece of paper and display their thoughts on it. It was uncomfortable for them for a while, but they saw the value of doing so when they went through real interview sessions successfully.

If you have news to deliver or something important to say to your staff, be sure you know not only "what" you want to say but also "how" you are going to say it.

Write it down. See if it's really clear. If so, good; if not, rewrite it, and try again.

Two roads diverged in a wood, and . . .
I took the one less traveled by,
And that has made all the difference.

Robert Frost
"The Road Not Taken"

This is one of the most often quoted lines of poetry ever penned.

The poem from which it is drawn is about decisions and consequences. And make no mistake about it—every decision we make has consequences. Further, we are responsible for those decisions and must live with those consequences.

There is a constant chain reaction involved. Decisions lead to consequences, which produce new conditions, which require new decisions, which have new consequences—and on and on.

Anyone who manages others has to be aware of the consequences of his actions and the impact of his decisions.

Everything we do leads to the next decision point, and every decision we make affects the lives of many others. So we must take the responsibility seriously, and make the decisions carefully and deliberately. Once made, a decision can't be unmade. Time has passed, and conditions have changed. Everything is different from what it was.

What we do as managers has far-reaching implications for many of those around us. So we must take our role responsibly, and make our choices carefully.

Read the entire poem if you haven't read it, and reread it if you have. A little bit of thought and a little bit of time spent in that "yellow wood" Frost wrote about might give you a few good ideas about how to do your job better for yourself and for others.

I am not a bit anxious
about my battles.
If I am anxious I don't fight them.
I wait until I am ready.
                    Field Marshal Sir Bernard Montgomery

When I first read this quotation I remembered thinking how simple this philosophy is and how obvious it is. Then I thought a little more and considered how often that simple philosophy isn't carried out.

Most of us are quick to act in business situations. We want to fix or control things; we want to take command and charge into battle. The results of such haste, however, are often less than we would hope because we encounter unexpected problems and obstacles. These unforeseen problems distract us, and we waste time, talent, and resources adjusting and correcting.

We "do battle" with subordinates and supervisors, with clients and colleagues; and often we are unsure why there is a battle going on and who—if anyone—is going to win it.

The lesson is simple, and yet the concept is profound: When we must perform, whether fighting a battle or giving a speech, we must not begin until we are ready to begin.

While watching the women's figure skating finals at the Winter Olympics years ago I was struck by something the commentators said as a sixteen-year-old skater was warming up. After she had practiced a few turns and jumps, she went over to the sideboards and just stood still. She was focusing on what was ahead and what she had to do. The commentator said, "Look at her. She won't begin until she's ready." Millions of viewers around the world were waiting and watching, but she didn't begin her performance until she was ready to begin.

If we took that kind of time to get ready and focused on what we must do with our lives, we would all make fewer errors, and we would all be much less anxious about our performance.

She won the gold medal.

So can we.

It is fatal to enter any war
without the will to win it.
General Douglas MacArthur

This is a rather extreme statement in a book on business-related topics and behaviors, but it gets our attention. In business we don't deal with battles and wars, but we do contend with projects, timetables, and competition. And often we either succeed or fail in accomplishing our tasks based on our will or lack of will.

Take this idea off the battlefield and put it in the business world. Without the will, the drive, the desire, and the sense of urgency to be successful, we will almost certainly fail. If failure is almost a certainty, then why begin in the first place?

Time and resources are limited, so they must be allocated where they can be most effective. As for the people involved, without commitment there will be little drive, which will result in poor performance. Again, why begin?

We can't win every battle we fight in business any more than we can close every contract we develop, but if we are determined to succeed, we will pick our battles and evaluate our options. Only then should we pursue the ones we are most passionate about.

Passion leads to energy, energy leads to resourcefulness, resourcefulness leads to options, and options lead to appropriate paths.

You can't do everything, so identify what is most important and focus on that one thing.

And then act—with a will!

**Practice doesn't make perfect—
practice makes
permanent!**

The opening statement that practice doesn't make perfect is probably contrary to what we have heard all our lives. Therefore, it's an uncomfortable thought. But when we think of the rest of the sentence, it makes perfect sense.

If we practice doing something the wrong way, no matter how often we repeat the behavior it will never get any better. Certainly it will never become perfect. Repetition, however, does lead to comfort, and because we do what is comfortable for us, we'll do it again and again.

If a behavior isn't productive, however, we need to change it. We shouldn't continue to repeat it, hoping for a better result.

Here's an example. A colleague of mine always saw himself as an effective communicator. In his mind's eye he was very clear in what he wanted done and quite efficient in his use of time. In his desire to to be efficient and effective there was an instance when he was sending out handwritten messages to his direct reports. E-mail didn't exist at the time, or he would have used it. His messages said, "See me." He signed the notes with his initials, GCC. Very crisp; very concise; very quick.

When one of his staff received this man's first message, his immediate reaction was, "I must have done something wrong." Before he went to see the boss he gathered all the documentation he could think of to explain his activities or justify any perceived shortcomings.

When he went to see him, his boss asked, "Can you and your wife come to dinner Friday night?" That's why he sent the "See me" message—to extend an invitation. He sent the same kind of messages many times to many people, and the results were always the same. The immediate reaction was, "I must have done something wrong." It was a bad reaction, and the repetition didn't make it any better.

Finally, his staff told him how they were reacting, and he stopped sending the curt messages. The longer he sent out "See me" messages, the more difficult it was for him to break the habit, but he did it.

Any bad habits you should break?

Silence
is
golden!

Old saying

All too often we talk when we should be quiet. Many of us are so enamored with the sound of our own voices we "sound off" when we should "shut up."

Even in situations where we know we should remain silent, we are often tricked—or seduced—into conversation. It seems that when someone expresses an interest in what we think, we give in and talk—even when we know we shouldn't.

Here is an interesting example that took place in a television studio a few years ago. The mother of a well-known controversial politician was asked a series of questions by the program host. A pleasant rapport had been established between the two women when the host leaned forward in her chair and in a faux whisper said, "Just between you and me, what do you think your son meant when he said . . . ?"

The rest of the quote isn't necessary here, but the guest volunteered some rather private and personal information about her son. She should have known there was no "you and me" but rather millions of viewers who heard her answer.

She should have remained quiet and not answered the "private" question.

This kind of thing happens in business settings often when a coworker asks for a "just between us guys" reaction to a company policy, boss, or process.

When that happens to you, avoid answering, because you have no idea where that information will go. The questioner may not have ulterior motives at the moment, but no one knows what subsequent moments might produce. Stay quiet if you can't be sure of the security of your answer.

You're running too great a risk to take a chance.

It's more important to
be good
than to
feel good.

Doing what feels good causes many business people to act in inappropriate ways—ways that often get them into trouble.

A few years ago I worked with a man who was let go from his position at a large company. Not unexpectedly, he was hurt by the decision and worried about his future.

The decision to terminate him wasn't made because of poor performance, but because of budget shifts and changing priorities. We have all faced those kinds of decisions in one way or another because they are a fact of life in business today.

Unfortunately, this man let his anger get the best of him, and in his exit interview he gave both his immediate supervisor and the Human Resources Department a "piece of his mind."

He told them exactly what he thought they could do with the job and with the entire company. His frustration overcame his better sense, but at the moment he felt good—very good—about speaking his mind. In fact, he felt great! And former coworkers let him know how inspired they were by what he had said and done.

Those exit interview comments, however, lived with his ex-boss and with the vice president of the HR department even after another position opened up the following week for which the departing employee would have been a "shoo-in." He was the best person they could have hired—and he would have been hired in an instant—under other circumstances.

But he didn't get the job. He didn't even get a call to discuss it.

Because he acted to "feel good," and it worked for a short time, his life was changed forever. All he had to do was to continue to be a good professional, and he would still be with that company.

He made a bad choice and is living to regret it.

By the way, all those former coworkers who told him how inspiring he was are still on the job.

In the land of the blind,
the one-eyed man is king.

Marshall Mcluhan

Everything must be viewed in context and in relation to other factors and conditions.

In this motto the one-eyed man is seen as fortunate and even as exceptional in a certain location. He is special, gifted, even revered.

If, however, the location changes, he might be viewed as unfortunate, limited, or inadequate.

The man is the same, but the surroundings are different.

Every one of us has talents—and limitations—and it's important to put them into a context.

Don't let the context dictate your behavior.

In all that you do, be sure to look carefully at the situation, and then resolve to use the talents you have. Then use them! Identify what you can do, and focus on the positive.

For most of us, this requires developing a firm positive attitude about our abilities. It seems easier for many of us to fixate on our limitations and then feel sorry for ourselves.

A close friend demonstrated this principle for me recently. He has been diagnosed with a rather severe illness. Because of the illness he can no longer do much of what previously had been commonplace for him.

But he said, "I know someday I'm going to die with this illness, but I won't die from it." Talk about a positive spin on a bad situation!

Since the diagnosis, he has begun to explore new opportunities and activities. His life is now different, but it's still full.

His context has changed, but he is still the same person. The only difference is he is now living in a new "land." And he's doing very well.

**Others never know
how you *feel*—
they only know
how you *behave*.**

People form opinions or make judgments about us by what we do. At first glance there seems to be stock placed on what we say and how we say it, but those impressions pale into insignificance compared to behavior.

We've all heard comments about people who "talk a good line," but that's never a compliment! Rather, it usually means a person is dishonest or not to be trusted.

Behavior is observable; it's powerful; and it's easy to understand. Feelings are internal, but behavior is external—it's open for all to observe.

The message for all of us here is clear. It may be easy to say yet difficult to carry out, but here it is. Do the right thing!

Most of us know what the "right thing" is, and we know what we should do.

We hear about what is right to do for our customers, for our colleagues, for our families, and for our communities, but we don't always do what we should.

Whenever you are faced with a difficult decision, ask yourself this simple question: "What is the right thing to do?" Then demand that you provide yourself with an honest answer.

When you "do the right thing," you'll be seen and judged on facts not on feelings. Those facts are clear to everyone, but the feelings may be confusing, wrong, and misunderstood. That's never a good way to conduct business or manage a staff.

Just do the right thing!

**Elegance
without warmth
is arrogance.**

Ritz Carlton Hotels

This motto of an upscale hotel chain sets the standard for customer service and satisfaction throughout the entire business community.

Their credo, which everyone in the organization believes and follows, is demonstrated in a single sentence:

"We are ladies and gentlemen serving ladies and gentlemen."

That single sentence defines the relationship that exists between every employee and every guest.

Imagine: An entire philosophy summed up in nine words!

Try doing that with your corporate philosophy and mission statement.

Then try doing it with your personal and professional mission statements.

What credo summarizes your life and work?

Often common sense isn't common practice.

Be careful whenever you hear anyone say that something is "common sense." Many people respond very differently when they hear that comment, feeling the need to explain their actions and positions. Sometimes the comment produces defensiveness and hesitancy.

It may be true that many things seem to be common sense, but many of those same things aren't performed under the banner of common sense. They simply aren't common practice, and the practice—the performance—is what's important.

What people do and how they behave is much more important and much more informative than what someone else "feels" about them or their actions.

So, as a first line of defense when you hear this criticism, just put the comment in perspective by acknowledging to yourself and others that, while it may be common sense, it doesn't always lead to common practice.

It is better to give
than to receive.

Paraphrase of the Apostle Paul
in Acts 20:35

The best way to put this line into context is to recognize why it's better to give.

That ability demonstrates clearly the simple fact that we are able to give—that we have been given the talents, the gifts, and the abilities to share with others.

Most of us have "inherited" what we have. It has come to us, not because of our actions, but because of the actions of others.

Now, I know full well that most of us have worked hard to achieve positions of success, but without the initial gifts we received from others there would be little, if anything, to develop.

A great athlete practices hard to hone his talents and abilities, but he didn't earn those talents and abilities. They were gifts from someone else.

Share what you have with others. The gifts you inherited from those who went before you can be passed on to those who will follow you.

Those "gifts" don't have to be things or dollars. Those wouldn't even be appropriate in many business settings. The gifts in the business world can and should be honesty, support, encouragement, assistance, guidance, and other such intangibles. Feel free to add to this list.

As a business leader, you have many gifts. Acknowledge the fact that you are in a position to pass them on to others. What you give to them just might be passed on to others, and others, and others.

That's a heady thought.

Try it.

Get ready.
Get set.
Go!

This saying sounds the same today as it did when we were kids. However, there is a big difference for some of us between then and now. When we were kids, we followed this sequence: First we would get ready (to run, to hide, etc.), then we would get set (assume the right posture, position, etc.), and finally we would go (start off at the designated sign or signal).

Unfortunately, today we often act before we are ready and set to act!

The pressures of time, economics, schedules, budgets, and other variables often result in action rather than thought. We act before we are adequately prepared. Too many times we find ourselves in the position of apologizing or explaining why we did something without thinking it through.

Your staff and your customers look to you for leadership and direction. And they look for consistency and stability. Taking quick action may sometimes seem expedient, but speed may produce errors and cause confusion. Having to make corrections will usually require much more time than was "saved" by a quick decision.

Since all the actions you take affect your staff, and by extension their work and their families, take your time. Ask questions to be sure you identify the issues and opportunities involved. Be certain you respond to the correct situations and not the first ones that come to mind.

The order is important: First, get ready; then, get set; finally, *go!*

Be careful what you ask for—
you just might get it.

Old saying

Before we get something new or do something new, everything about it looks good to us. Most things look good at a distance because we can't see the details from far away. It's only when we get up close that we see the blemishes.

Certainly, viewing from a distance can be beneficial because it helps us to determine a general direction and to plot a tentative course. The difficulty, however, comes when that long view gives way to the clear view of every bump in the road. A mountain from far away doesn't look threatening, but up close it's a very different story.

The same caution applies to the workplace. The jobs and the responsibilities others have look interesting—and often easy. So they become attractive to us. When we take on that new job and those new responsibilities, though, all the specific conditions may be quite different.

So when you seek out and bid for a new position, be sure you've done your homework in advance. Know what you're getting into. Talk to your predecessor on the job and to your future colleagues if at all possible. Get a ground-level, close-up picture rather than relying on the bird's-eye view.

Once you get "it," it's yours. Be sure "it" is what you want before you take it.

We judge ourselves
by our intentions,
but we judge others
by their behaviors.

U.S. Supreme Court

All of us look at ourselves with a biased set of eyes. Every image we have is filtered by what we think we are and by how we think we appear to others. That image is distorted, but it is one we have to live with every day.

No one else on earth can see us as we see ourselves. We know every intimate detail about ourselves—our desires, our drives, our motives, our expectations, and our intentions.

But very few of us live in isolation, and we constantly interact with others—others who also see themselves in their own unique ways.

Therefore, we act and react toward others based not on what they feel inside but on the basis of how they behave, and on the basis of what they do.

People in every business and every walk of life know what they want to happen, what their motives are, and what they want to achieve.

Consider your own life and your own motives. You know what you want from yourself, and you know what you want and expect from others. But, all of those other people respond to you solely on the basis of how you act toward them. They don't know what you feel inside.

They can't get inside you and touch your "feelings buttons"; they know only what you do to, with, and for them.

Try an "out of body" experience sometime and view yourself as others view you. It's private, so be honest!

What do you see? Is it the picture you want to see?

Fix it, or preserve it. It's your choice—and your responsibility.

**People don't care about
how you *feel*.
They care about
how you *act*.**

When you are responsible for any group of people—a company, a department, or a family—one of your primary roles is to be a teacher. Because you can't do everything yourself, you have to help others learn how to contribute.

When people in business settings do this, it's called "delegating," and delegating is an important business skill.

But, here's the problem. Many managers think that delegating simply means telling others what to do. Delegation requires careful selection and observation of the tasks and the people who are to perform them. It requires helping those people understand why they were selected for the task, and then providing them the instruction they need in order to do what is expected of them.

Then there are two more tasks—tasks that are often overlooked or taken for granted: Be sure these people have all the tools and resources necessary to carry out the delegated tasks, and then monitor their progress. Monitoring doesn't mean looking over their shoulder, second-guessing, and checking on every specific action they take.

Once you have defined and described the goal, step back. The delegated persons may select a different route to achieve the goal, but that's okay. You may have your way of doing something, but that doesn't mean it's the only way.

The way you act toward the people who work for you, and the way you delegate tasks can establish a work environment that will be either beneficial or restrictive for everyone involved.

Set the standard. Establish a supportive environment. Delegate duties and responsibilities. Then let your workers do their jobs.

**When all else fails,
read the directions.**

Wife to husband

This motto doesn't relate only to hooking up a computer or pro-gramming a VCR. It means taking the time to learn how something functions before attempting to operate it. This necessity is obvious with every work-related group you'll encounter. It involves learning about the behaviors that will be acceptable to the group.

Groups all demonstrate specific collective behaviors called "norms." A norm is what a group *does,* and in the workplace such actions may or may not conform to stated company practices or policies.

For example, company policy might state that the workday runs from nine to five. That's clear, and the expectation is that all employ-ees will actually be working during those hours. That's what they're being paid to do.

However, the norm in the company might be different. It might be that everyone is there at nine, but first they get a cup of coffee or tea, then chat about the early morning news, check their personal e-mail, and set up lunch plans. When they start working, it's nine-twenty.

Ten to fifteen minutes before noon, their desks are straightened up, and work stops in order to get ready for lunch. Toward the end of the day, business slows down again, and employees discuss and confirm evening plans.

This norm allows everyone to waste almost an hour every day! None of that behavior is promoted anywhere, but it's what every-one does.

When you have difficulty getting things done and getting staff to work properly, read the signs, check your directions, and watch the behaviors (the norms). Group norms are much more powerful than any corporate policy!

If at first you don't succeed,
try,
try again.

Common saying

That's right! Keep trying, but don't keep doing the same thing the same way over and over again. If something doesn't work, it's because you're doing it wrong.

Doing the same thing the same way hundreds of times won't make it any better. It will just make it more comfortable because you've developed a new habit. Habits feel good so you repeat the behavior. But repetition doesn't necessarily result in improvement.

Here's an analogy that a colleague and I used in a book on managing. We said that one of the roles of a successful manager is to behave like an accomplished gardener. A good gardener makes many choices—just as a good manager does. The gardener picks the soil, the seeds, the water, the light, and so forth.

If all the elements are combined properly and tended to diligently, in time the plants will grow. And then, of course, they will require further attention and care. If the plants don't grow, the gardener would be foolish to do everything the same way again! He will change the soil, or the water, or the light, or the fertilizer, or whatever it takes to find the right combination of elements.

He knows that repeating what didn't work in the first place will only result in further failure and disappointment. So he finds what will work.

Managing requires the same attention, the same focus, and the same flexibility in identifying the business equivalents of the seeds, the soil, the moisture, the light, and the other variables.

Here's something else to consider for your business garden.

What should do you do with the weeds?

**When you discover
you're digging yourself
into a hole—
stop digging.**

The first time I heard this comment my reaction was, "That is brilliant! It's funny; it's graphic; it's simple; and it makes sense!"

It needs little—if any—explanation. But here is one anyway.

Many of us find ourselves doing our jobs in the same way over and over again. If conditions change, but we don't, those repeated behaviors produce less than desirable results. Our reaction to that situation is, "It worked before, so it should work now." We keep doing the same thing in the same way—and conditions keep getting worse and worse.

The longer we continue the repeated unproductive behaviors, the worse conditions get.

So, what should we do? The answer is simple: stop!

If something you're doing just doesn't work anymore, find another way.

Remember this simple direction about digging yourself into a hole. It's funny—but it's true.

Nature abhors
a vacuum.

Benedict Spinoza

This truth is demonstrated in business every day. Not in the scientific sense, of course, but in an operational sense.

Every business consists of multiple people interacting in various settings. Those people are constantly reacting to the changing conditions around them. Those reactions are an attempt to adjust in order to maintain a certain sense of balance. One of the necessary ingredients for that balance is information. Workers want to know, "What's up? What's going on? What's happening?"

Because a vacuum can't perpetuate itself, here's what happens as soon as information ceases to flow. The involved participants make it up!

When information doesn't come from the top of an organization, others elsewhere create their own truth. It may start out as a simple, "I think . . . ," or "I heard . . . ," but in short order the created facts take on a life of their own. And they grow strong and fast.

Those facts have many names: "scuttlebutt," "skinny," "the latest," but they are all manufactured, and, most of the time, they're wrong! But you can be sure they'll be made up to fill any void in the information flow.

The lesson here for all of us in business settings is this: When you have information, share it with your colleagues—if at all possible. Obviously there will be some times when certain data must remain confidential, but be sure there is a need rather than just a preference.

That way, even if the facts are unpleasant, they are at least facts. It's always a lot easier to deal with facts than with fiction.

Give a man a fish,
and he'll eat for a day.
Teach a man to fish,
and he'll eat for a lifetime.

Chinese proverb

This saying relates to short-term versus long-term activities. Certainly there is good reason for giving an item, but there is a different reason for providing a skill. Both are good, but each must be selected purposefully.

Many managers were promoted to their positions because they were good "doers." They could do something well. Usually, they got so good at "doing" they were rewarded by being moved to a managerial position.

Without further support and instruction, that's the same as giving a man a fish. He'll use it and use it, but in time it will be gone. A manager who doesn't grow doesn't succeed, and his failure doesn't help a company or a department.

Because his information and resources are limited—like a single fish—he will remain a "doer"; he will just have a different title.

We've all seen the "doer" manager in action. As soon as something goes wrong, he jumps in and fixes it. Subordinates and staff members are pushed out of the way while the "doer" addresses the situation.

A true manager learns to fish—in other words, he learns an entirely new set of skills. He acquires, practices, and perfects new behaviors that were not required in his prior position.

When you promote someone to this important position, be sure you provide both the skills and the knowledge that will be necessary for success.

If you are the one who has been promoted, but you haven't been taught what you need to know to be successful in that new position, take a few fishing lessons!

I don't want to give you the impression
that I don't have faith in God in the air.
It is just that I have more experience
with him on the ground.

Martin Luther King Jr.

I met Dr. Martin Luther King Jr. on a stormy night in Connecticut just a few weeks before he accepted the Nobel Prize. He was the guest of honor at a gathering, but he was late arriving because of a bad storm that delayed his flight.

When he finally arrived, he apologized and said the trip was a bit frightening. He said he was glad when the plane landed safely. When there was a little chuckle from the assembled group, he stopped his opening remarks and made that interesting statement.

I've thought of that evening and that sentence often because it serves as a kind of reality check.

We all look for our own comfort level in business and personal situations, and that's where we usually perform best. If, however, Dr. King had not been in the air earlier that evening he would not have been at the meeting. Distance would have prevented his attendance.

We plan, and we place our trust in others in business, and sometimes that trust requires a leap of faith. But that's okay.

Dr. King's words summarize an all-important business concept.

Business is all about building relationships, and his relationship spoke for itself in that one sentence.

So should ours.

**When you care enough
to send the very best.**

Hallmark Cards

This motto is obviously a well-known identifier of a very successful U.S. company. It creates an image of quality as well as social grace. It reflects something that is important.

As business people, we can and should take a lesson about demonstrating and recognizing importance. If or when you are in a position to offer a significant promotion to someone in your company, acknowledge it as an important event. It is always significant when someone moves up to a higher position on the organization chart.

It is interesting that when a person is promoted to a vice president level or higher, for example, it is usually seen and treated as a "big deal." And it should be!

Not only is there a new office, and maybe a reserved parking spot, there is also a press release for the local papers, a dinner or cocktail party, perhaps even some kind of souvenirs. And that is all good!

But what is done to and for the lower-level person who is promoted to his first manager position? Usually nothing. And that is not good!

It's a "big deal" to that person, so it should be celebrated. When you promote someone, host a luncheon that includes the person's spouse. Send out a press release. Make it an important event in the company and community, because it is important to the new manager.

This celebration doesn't have to be expensive or elaborate. It simply should be observable.

The long-term results of such a celebration will be well worth the investment.

'Tis pride
that pulls
the country down.

Shakespeare
Othello

In an everyday business organization the things that are "pulled down" by pride are the structure and the reputation of the company.

When selfishness rather than service takes hold in an organization, emphasis shifts, and actions become counterproductive. Decisions are made that benefit and profit only a few, while multitudes suffer and pay the price.

There have been many examples of this phenomenon in recent years, the most notable of course being Enron and Global Crossing. So strong was the fallout of the actions of a few that the companies crumbled. Both company names are now associated with deceit and failure. And they deserve to be.

Misplaced pride caused the disasters.

As business people, we should be proud of our work, and we can show that pride by putting the customers and the products first. If we produce quality products and provide quality services, while applying sound business practices, success will follow in terms of growth and profit.

If we focus only on ourselves, we will become shortsighted. Business demands taking a long view and paying attention to customers. This sounds simple, but the most important element in any business is the customer.

When the customer goes away, so does the business. When a company loses that simple relationship, its days are numbered.

Put the emphasis in the right place. Remember the words Marshall Field spoke when he set the philosophy of his very successful stores: "Give the lady what she wants." It still works.

**A hard beginning
maketh
a good ending.**

John Heywood
Proverb

Often, what makes a project difficult to complete is the fact the initial steps were faulty or hesitant. In order to succeed we must prepare, learn, and perhaps acquire new skills and techniques.

When I was very young my family moved from the heart of the city to a new suburban development. It was very nice, but very different from what anyone in the family had ever experienced.

I remember it became clear we needed a garage. None of the new houses had a garage, so my father decided to build one—himself—with some help from his young son. This was a brand-new undertaking. It was going to be hard to do, and it certainly had some risks attached. But here's what happened.

My father sent me to the library (this was long before the Internet) with this simple direction: "Pick up some books about building things like garages."

As I recall, I brought back six or seven books for him, and he began to read, and to draw, and to measure, and to read some more. I don't remember exactly how long this went on, but it was a long time.

Finally, he said, "Okay. It's time." We went out to the yard, drove some stakes into the ground, and ran string from stake to stake. Then we dug a hole for the foundation, mixed concrete, and built walls with cinder blocks. Finally we had a garage! And it was a very good garage. It's still standing, and there isn't a crack in it anywhere.

Whenever I see it, it's a testimony and a memorial in one structure.

It was hard work getting started, but the end product was worth the effort.

Whether you're building a garage, a department, or a company, the principle is the same: A good beginning ensures a successful ending.

**Nothing is impossible
to a
willing heart.**

John Heywood
Proverb

Describing acts of heroism that happen every day—unknown to most people—is the easiest way to expand on this motto. Ordinary heroes do what they do because they want to do it. No one is watching—or evaluating. They simply act. They do what is necessary.

But, here is the initial ingredient of such action. In their own minds, what they do is worth doing. They act to achieve a goal. Sometimes the goal is instantly visible and achievable, and other times it requires careful planning and practice.

Consider what you want to accomplish in your career. Write down your goal. The act of writing, by the way, is important because you won't be able to write it if it isn't truly clear in your mind.

You can fool yourself, but you can't fool a blank piece of paper.

Next, determine what you have to do to accomplish that goal, and then commit to doing what is necessary.

Long days, no vacation, low pay, extended travel, difficult courses, whatever it takes.

When you commit, you'll achieve.

You might not be the "hero" whose picture ends up in the newspaper and on TV, but you'll have accomplished your goal.

When you're willing to work toward a goal, you'll reach it.

If you could see her
through my eyes . . .

"If You Could See Her"
Cabaret

This motto is from the lyrics of a song in a musical play. The bitter-sweet song, I think, epitomizes how we can all create our own reality.

The way we see conditions often leads to the creation of those conditions. It's a spin on the concept of the self-fulfilling prophecy. If we concentrate on seeing the good in our colleagues—or our children—we will, by example, encourage them to succeed.

Pick out an employee, delegate tasks to that individual, provide the necessary tools and resources, and that person will probably perform to your expectation.

Educators are familiar—or should be—with what psychologists call the Pygmalion Effect. Research studies have demonstrated that when teachers expect their students to do well, they do. When teachers don't expect their students to do well, that too, is exactly what happens!

Attitudes drive behaviors.

For many years I was a member of the faculty of Northwestern University. It is a great university, and even though it is part of the Big Ten Conference, its football team left much to be desired. In fact, it was sort of a joke—until a new coach entered the picture. His philosophy was simple, and it was reflected in posters and banners throughout the practice field and in the locker room. Two words said it all: "Expect Victory."

A lot of people joked about it—said it would never happen. But, after a lot of hard work, the Northwestern football team won the Big Ten championship and went to the Rose Bowl.

They didn't win the game at the Rose Bowl, but they got there.

First they saw it. Then they reached it.

If she seem not chaste to me,
What care I how chaste she be?
                              Sir Walter Raleigh

This is a clear description of the egocentric personality.

It's another way of saying, "I know what I like, and I like what I know." Or "My mind's made up; don't confuse me with facts." A colleague gave me a wonderful example of this truth recently. Here's what she said.

"I had the opportunity to work with a senior manager who had just joined the company I had worked with for fifteen years.

"At the national sales meeting, the new manager unveiled a new program offering she had developed. However, there was a big problem. When the sales force saw her new product, there was universal shock. What this new manager proposed was diametrically opposed to everything that had made the company successful for more than three decades.

"The sales force became vocal about their displeasure. Hearing that, and attempting to justify her position, the new manager said, 'Well, during the six months I've been with the company I have seen . . .' There was another strong negative reaction to the comment about 'six months' when everyone else had much more relevant experience over a much longer term."

This manager thought she knew what needed to be done, but she reached her conclusions based on very limited information. In her mind, she concluded what she thought was "truth." Since she thought it, she was convinced it must be true.

This is a dangerous conclusion for anyone to reach.

Her situation hasn't been resolved yet. As another old saying goes, "Only time will tell," but this was a rocky start for a new phase of that company—and for that manager.

Before you speak or act, make sure you're seeing clearly and accurately.

All the world's a stage,
and all the men and women
merely players.

Shakespeare
As You Like It

In other words, we all have our roles to play. However, although there are similarities between the actors' roles and our various roles as business people, there are also significant differences.

Let's take a look at both of them. First the similarities. Actors have things to say and things to do. They have specific personalities that influence their words and actions and the words and actions of everyone else in the cast. The behavior of each actor influences the reactions of others and the direction of the story line. That's true in business too.

As for the differences, the author determines the actors' words and actions, but in business, we determine the words and actions. We are all free to make choices, but actors don't have that flexibility. That flexibility means that each of us is responsible not only for our own words and actions, but also for considering the impact our words and actions might have on others around us.

Now here's the huge difference between actors and business people. Business people don't have a script! We can't blame a writer for giving us poor lines or poor action. On the other hand, we are not constrained by those either. Because we write the script and act out the part, we control what happens throughout our daily "play."

Finally, there isn't a conclusion to the play in which we speak and act. There are a series of acts, and what we say and do during our time on the stage determines what others who follow us will say and do. There is never a curtain call or an encore, but we can work toward audience appreciation and even, perhaps, a loud "Bravo."

It isn't difficult
when you
want to do it.

An elderly gentleman

An aunt of mine told me this story of an elderly man in the nursing facility where she worked many years ago. The man ate only kosher food, and one day she commented to him that it must be difficult to follow such strict dietary regulations.

He looked a little surprised when she said that, and he responded, "I've done this all my life. This is my life. I have never thought of following any other diet.

"I want to do this, and nothing is difficult when you *want* to do it."

What clear focus, and what strong conviction.

As we work through our careers with their highs and lows, we should keep that man's comment in mind. If we have truly found our calling in what we are doing, we will do all that is necessary to be successful.

Long hours, difficult conditions, harsh challenges will all be taken in stride because they come with the job. If we concentrate on the mission, we will accept the challenges as opportunities, and we will carry out what is expected of us, not because we have to but because we want to.

It is incredible what people can accomplish when there is desire and commitment. For strong examples and role models of commitment and desire, think of the military in time of war, and think of the men and women who gave so much in New York City on September 11, 2001. By comparison, the jobs we are now doing probably seem pretty easy.

Remember: Where there is the desire to do, there is the will to fulfill.

Men's evil manners
live in brass;
their virtues
we write in water.

Shakespeare
King Henry VIII

I thought of this line from Shakespeare recently when I was in a cleaners to pick up a suit. There was a sign over the cash register that put this thought in words more common today. The sign said, "No one remembers the good things I do, but no one ever forgets when I make a mistake."

This seems to be a sad commentary. It's unfair, but it is a fact of life for many of us. That means we all have to be aware of the bad judgments we make. The problems we create leave almost indelible marks on our careers and on our colleagues' perceptions of us. Often, those actions are unintentional, but they still exist, and they create reactions.

In most instances it is just as easy to do the "right thing" as it is to do the "wrong thing." Whichever course of action we take will have an impact on us and on those around us.

As early as possible in your career, decide how you want to be perceived, thought of, and remembered by your colleagues and associates. This isn't intended as a eulogy or as an epitaph but simply as a way to establish in your own mind the kind of person you want to be, the kind of manager you want to be, the kind of spouse and parent you want to be. When you've made those decisions, do what is necessary to construct and preserve that image.

Whatever you do will be remembered and recorded either in brass or in water. Of course the brass lasts longer than the water, so do more of the good than the bad to keep the image strong.

Fortune brings in
some boats
that are not steered.

Shakespeare
Cymbeline

Every once in a while we succeed out of just plain luck.

This quotation caught my attention because I have been involved with boats for many years. As all boaters know, it takes a great deal of skill, care, experience, and patience to operate a boat well.

Planning and caution are always essential in order to avoid catastrophe. A friend of mine who operates a marina told me a great story about a man who wanted to rent a boat from him. My friend called off the rental when he was going over the boat with the renter prior to casting off when the renter asked him where the brake pedal was!

It would be a long stretch to expect that rental boat to come back safely to port. Fortune and good luck might do it, but no one can or should depend on those.

In our business relationships, and in personal relationships in general, sometimes we may see events come to positive conclusions through sheer luck and good fortune alone. But, we shouldn't count on it.

In all of our dealings with customers and colleagues we must pay attention to the human counterparts of wind, tide, currents, and depth. We must plan a course of action and react to changes in the conditions. Most important, when we cast off, we need to know where we are headed and how to get there safely. In business we need to know what we want to accomplish and how to achieve it.

Think of your market as a large body of water, your product or service as a worthy vessel, and cast off.

If it were done . . .
then 'twere well
it were done quickly.

Shakespeare
Macbeth

I have a good friend who, like many people, has dreams, plans, aspirations, talents, and desires; but he lacks a certain vital ingredient: Drive!

Until he gets it, he will be limited in the success he can expect. Too often, and for too long, he has been the victim of "What if . . ." thinking.

Now, usually the expression "What if . . ." signals dreams, creativity, and exploration. In fact, many companies use it as a management tool and conduct seminars to encourage "out-of-the-box" thinking. And it works!

With my friend, however, the same expression works to lead him down a very different path. Even when he has a sound idea or a dream, he'll say, "But what if I can't do it? What if this doesn't work? What if they laugh at me? What if I don't get the job or the promotion?"

The same two words "What if" lead him in a different direction. Rather than being energized by possibilities, my friend is paralyzed by uncertainty. As a result, he has talked himself out of implementing many good ideas over the years.

The lesson for all of us is simple: Begin! Business roads and careers are strewn with "What if" wrecks. Don't contribute to the collection.

Begin! Set a plan, and then do something. You won't be careless because you will have made a plan. You know how to begin. If you don't succeed for some reason, figure out what the reason was, revise your plan, and begin again.

Ask yourself this question: "What if I'm successful; what then?"

When I fool
the people I fear
I fool myself as well!

> Anna in "I Whistle a Happy Tune"
> *The King and I*

This quotation doesn't mean that bluffing is a substitute for competing. It reflects the relationship between behavior and perception that Jack Grossman and I described in our recent book, *Becoming a Successful Manager*.

No one can ever know how we truly feel about anything. Observers, audiences, and coworkers make judgments about us solely on the basis of what we say or do. No one can know if we are confident, frightened, or insecure inside. They can only draw conclusions based on the way we speak or act on the outside. If we are really scared to death, no one will ever know because they might be observing something quite different, and that's what counts!

When we behave in a way that is perceived as being confident, our colleagues will likewise feel that confidence in us because of the model we are demonstrating. When that image is projected, it reflects back on us in as positive way.

If we stand up straight, look people in the eye, and use a strong voice even when we are afraid or anxious, those behaviors will begin to make us feel more confident and more assured of success. Of course, this image of confidence and success will become reality only if there is competence and ability to support the image.

Whenever you have to deal with staff, customers, or employees, think about the line from this song. Use the physical skills to project a strong positive image, and you'll probably surprise yourself not only by how well you perform but also by how good you feel about it.

**You can't solve a problem
with the same mindset
that got you into the problem
in the first place.**

Albert Einstein

Once again, Albert Einstein was right! I thought about this quotation recently when working with a client. His company was experiencing high turnover with entry-level employees.

Identifying, interviewing, selecting, and training new people to replace those leaving was driving him to distraction. He was frustrated to say the least, but he kept up the replacement process as best he could. He blamed the situation on all kinds of things—the schools, the candidates, the screening, etc.—as he repeated his "time-proven" busy routine.

It didn't occur to him that a large part of the problem he was having related to the way he was going about the task. He thought he knew what kind of person and training were necessary because he had been working at the company for a long time—and what he had done for years had always been successful in the past.

He didn't consider the changes that had taken place over the years. Technology, mobility, and flexibly had become more important factors in the people entering the work force. His "tried-and-true" method of past years didn't fit the new workforce.

He simply had to change his mindset. There was nothing "wrong" with the people or the conditions, but they were different from those he had selected in the past. By failing to recognize those differences, he had created his own problem.

Once he shifted his mental gears and looked carefully at what was true now rather than in the past, he modified his recruiting, selecting, and training. As a result, his problems went away.

That kind of change in mindset should be a lesson to all of us.

Leadership and
learning are
indispensable
to each other.

John F. Kennedy
November 22, 1963

In order to be a leader, the first step you must take is to be a learner.

Without knowledge, actions are based on guesswork. That's risky. In fact, even good guessing requires some kind of information on which to base the guess. A guess is about something, and even a cursory glance at that something will yield a bit of information.

What do you need to learn in order to be an effective leader in your business? The list can be quite long. Of course, you need to learn about your product or service. That's obvious. Then you must learn about your customers and clients. What do they really want, need, expect? How do they feel about you and your company? What experiences have they had with others in your company—or with your competitors?

Who are those competitors? Can they offer anything you can't? If so, what? Why can't you offer it? What economic factors guide or control your business?

What do you know about the people working with you and for you? What about your superiors? What drives both your superiors and your subordinates?

Take time to learn before you attempt to lead. There are far too many people in business today who fill leadership and management positions but who lack knowledge, and as a result they usually make serious mistakes.

Leadership and knowledge are two sides of the same coin, and both are necessary for success.. Just as it's impossible to have a one-sided coin, it's impossible to be a true leader without accurate knowledge.

So if you want to be a leader, be a learner.

**If there isn't enough time
to do a job well—
how come there is always
enough time to do it over again?**

It seems everyone in the workplace—and in life in general—has this same complaint. There just isn't enough time! Without "enough time" we all seem to complete tasks in a "best we could do given the time constraints" manner. The job performance is okay, but it isn't first class.

The irony in this situation, though, lies in the fact that the "okay" task is later redone and becomes much better. There really was enough time. It was just a matter of allocation and sequencing. There was plenty of time to do the task over again.

Recently, I had a client who complained about the short time lines she had to produce reports for her board. She always waited until the last minute to get things organized, and then indeed got them done, but she found herself all too often apologizing for errors (most of which were minor, though some were major) and promising to forward corrected copies later. Obviously, this was a bad pattern, and it could have led to unpleasant consequences if it had continued too long.

The solution to her "problem" was to develop clear—and realistic—times for herself and for those who had to provide her with essential material. The "fix" involved and required commitment from many different parties. It was uncomfortable for many people for a while, but in time it became evident that the better planning resulted in improved accuracy with less stress and tension.

In short, her attention to time made life and work easier for everyone involved.

Do you have time to do your work well? If not, when will you have time to do it over again?

**Don't confuse activity
with achievement.**

This confusion can be seen in business settings every day. People at all levels are busy doing things, but too often they are accomplishing very little.

Sometimes the questionable activity is the result of a lack of worker focus, and sometimes it is faulty business procedures that encourage nonproductive activity.

Here is an example of each of those situations. First, let's examine the lack of employee focus. Look at the way offices and cubicles are arranged. Usually, from the outside it's difficult to see the screens of the omnipresent computers because of their placement relative to the doorway. The operator is "active," but the productivity is questionable because of the ever-increasing use of personal e-mail and Internet surfing during business hours.

Now let's consider the faulty business procedures. Many sales-related organizations require their sales people to make a certain number of phone calls to clients every day. They are measured, evaluated, and rewarded on the basis of the number of calls they make—or don't make.

That's the wrong measure! What is important is the number of *sales* made, not the number of *calls* made. Anyone in sales knows that extended conversations and contacts are necessary to produce results.

When managers assume that the number of calls is the primary determiner of success, they are simply playing the percentage game. If the sales people have to be monitored to be sure they are making a certain number of calls per day, maybe the managers hired the wrong people in the first place.

More important, such a focus might mean the wrong managers were hired!

As a manager, are you more interested in activity or achievement?

Be careful what you pretend—
because, in the end,
you will become what you pretend.

Kurt Vonnegut

This quotation sounds like a caution or an admonition because it seems to predict a negative outcome, but that doesn't have to be the end result. It all depends upon what we pretend. Here are a couple of examples.

When he started his career many years ago, a longtime friend of mine wanted to become a "hard-nosed business man." He had his own idea of what that role entailed, and he began acting the part— as he saw it.

He was critical, impatient, demanding, dictatorial, and he wasted little time on social and interpersonal activities. Actually, he was none of those things in his early years, but he pretended to be in order to become "successful."

Today, he is all of those things! But recently he confided to me that, at this stage of his life, he doesn't want to be that kind of person. In his own words, he doesn't like the person he has become.

He has engaged a personal executive coach to help him with his transformation. One of the initial steps in this process requires that he behave differently from his "usual" manner.

He is now acting more patient, and less critical, and he is behaving in ways that are more supportive and respectful of those around him. He is "pretending" again, but this time the actions are positive. He hopes the outcome will also be positive.

If he keeps working at this new role, he will become what he pretends to be. He knows this principle works; he did it once before, and he's confident he can do it again.

We all can become what we pretend. We just have to work at it.

**Optimism
creates
possibilities.**

Anyone who is truly interested in starting or developing a new business or moving into a new career must first believe he can become successful. Once a person takes that initial leap of faith, the next step is figuring out just how to do it.

That's true for all of us. It's like the children's book about "the little engine that could." I'm sure you remember the defining line in the book: "I think I can, I think I can, I think I can."

Here are just two examples of what hard work can accomplish after belief has set the stage.

The Wright brothers believed they could fly. That goal clearly was optimistic, but it was the necessary first step. Then they worked long and hard to identify exactly what they had to do to solve all the problems associated with achieving their goal. No optimism—no achievement.

Here's another one. A former business associate of mine opened a corner grocery store many years ago. It was successful, but he had loftier ideas, and he figured out how to turn that single corner store that he operated with his brother into one of the largest family-owned supermarket chains in the country.

First, he was optimistic, then he used his talent and experience to do what few others have been able to do. The chain, by the way, is still expanding.

The lesson is clear for all of us. Dream, believe, work, innovate, evaluate, modify.

But first, dream; or nothing will follow.

The choice of a point of view
is the initial act
of a culture.

Jose Ortegay Gasset

The culture of a workplace doesn't just happen. It is the result of what people do. Attitudes drive behaviors, and those behaviors create the mental environment called "culture."

It doesn't take long to determine whether a specific workplace is a good place to work. All you have to do is listen to what people are saying, and observe how they treat each other.

Do they help, guide, and support; or do they hinder, confuse, and criticize?

A manager has the power—and the responsibility—to deliberately create the culture under his control.

A manager can create a negative culture in which all of the workers watch out for themselves and distrust authority.

On the other hand, a manager can create a problem-solving culture in which everyone supports colleagues and moves toward achievement rather than correction.

As a manager, you must determine which culture you want to create for yourself and for everyone else who works with you and for you.

Here is a simple self-test that will help you follow one path or the other. Determine which kind of questions you ask. The answer will identify the culture you are creating.

Do you ask, "Why didn't we reach our numbers last quarter?" or do you ask, "What do we need to do to reach our numbers next quarter?"

One answer finds fault and creates mistrust; the other invites participation and provides direction.

Pick one.

A coward turns away,
but a brave man's choice
is danger.

Euripides

At first glance this seems to be an old-fashioned "swashbuckling" concept. Cowardice versus bravery is an age-old conflict, but, in business, we face these choices every day.

In our world, there aren't any flags and armor and weapons, but there are choices that require courage, strength, and fortitude.

Every time a manager must direct or discipline an employee, the differences between cowardice and strength are easy to see.

The cowardly manager avoids an unpleasant situation as best he can. His behavior of choice often includes sending an e-mail, leaving a phone message, or sometimes ignoring the situation, hoping it will just go away. Usually it doesn't. It just gets worse.

On the other hand, the brave manager faces the situation, assesses the conditions, selects a strategy, and then takes action.

Unlike a physical battle, however, the brave manager doesn't seek to win by vanquishing an enemy. The brave manager, the professional manager, works to help all parties to win.

The brave manager sees his role as both a leader and as a teacher. He "wins" when employees grow and develop, and when business thrives and progresses.

It takes courage and strength to teach and to lead. Cowards don't possess either of these qualities.

That's why they hold back, keep their heads down, and don't make waves.

Not a comfortable picture is it?

As a manager, are you cowardly or brave?

The great thing in this world
is not so much where we stand
as in what direction we are moving.
Oliver Wendell Holmes

A former associate of mine once operated a successful business. This is past tense because the business is no longer successful. He's still in it, but he has lost a significant share of his market. Here's why.

When he started, he looked for opportunities, and he took them. He opened new markets with new ideas and new services. That was the reason for his success. But the ideas and the services didn't remain "new." He kept doing what he knew how to do, and he did it in the way he knew worked for him—then.

Competitors saw his success, repeated it, and then improved upon what he had started. He continued to do what worked for him. He stood his ground!

He demonstrated that old comment, "I know what I like, and I like what I know."

For a while he retained his position in the market, but slowly and inevitably his competitors caught up with him and then moved ahead of him.

He still had a good product—but it was good for yesterday's market!

He remained solid in his convictions and in his business practices. Since the competition was moving forward, by comparison, he was moving backward. Today, his business is a fraction of what it once was, and it was his choices that made the difference.

Now, unless he changes, he can't catch up.

Movement is inevitable; progress is a choice.

Are you progressing, or are you simply moving?

To reach the port . . . . we must sail
sometimes with the wind
and sometimes against it—
but we must sail,
and not drift, nor lie at anchor.
Oliver Wendell Holmes

Three significant points are evident in this quotation.

To be successful as a manager in any business setting, we must have a goal; we must have knowledge; and we must have determination.

Just as the captain of a ship must know where he wants to go in order to plot a course, the manager or business leader needs a vision. He must know where he wants to take his company and his colleagues. Without a destination or a goal it's impossible to measure the value of an activity.

The activity, of course, must be based on knowledge. An accomplished sea captain knows about the vagaries of the winds, about water currents, about the characteristics of his vessel, and probably most important of all, he knows about the strengths and capabilities of his crew.

Finally, the sea captain must demonstrate the desire and will to move his vessel to new places by leaving the safety of the harbor.

The vision of the manager must be nourished by his knowledge of the marketplace and his competitors, and he must let his crew help him reach his goal. He must influence the crew with the will and the motivation to work to achieve that goal, because he can't do it alone.

Look at any successful business, and you'll see these three factors: a clear goal, good information, and focused action.

They all require energy. Success and safe passage, whether at sea or in business, are very rarely achieved by accident.

Don't just drift or lie at anchor; launch out into the deep and follow your planned course!

**Knowledge
should be his guide,
not
personal experience.**

Plato

This truth has become increasingly evident and critical in recent years in the business world. The constant movement of people within businesses has resulted in a phenomenon relatively unknown a generation ago.

Not many years back, it was common for people to get a job with a company and stay with that company until retirement. Such employees gained both experience and knowledge about their business because they devoted their entire working years to a single organization.

Today, people at all levels are constantly job-hopping every few years. This is particularly evident at many senior-level positions. The problems arise as it becomes clear that many of the senior executives rely on past experience in a former business rather than acquiring relevant information about the new business.

Some basic principles apply in many different businesses, but being successful requires more than general principles. It requires actively learning about the new environment. Success in one arena doesn't insure success in another. As a simple example, consider this sports analogy.

Winning is paramount in all sports competition, but the rules of all the games differ. You must know the rules of the game in order to play and win. You can't play quarterback on a baseball team!

When you have the opportunity to move to a new and exciting position for which you are qualified—take it. Then take the time to learn it. Don't rely solely on your past experiences.

Don't talk of love . . .
Show me!

Eliza Doolittle in "Show Me"
My Fair Lady

In the musical, *My Fair Lady,* a minor character named Freddy loudly proclaims his love for Eliza Doolittle when he sings "On the Street Where You Live." Because of a series of events we won't cover here Eliza responds to Freddy's profession with this quotation.

It's a great scene in the show, but it's also a profound truth for all business and managerial activities: "Don't just talk! Show me!"

Do something. Talk is cheap, but without action it means nothing.

In fact, when talk isn't backed up by action it's worse than silence. Here's an example from a company with which I've worked as a consultant.

There is a strong and valuable cadre of independent contractors who have been associated with the company for many years. They are valuable because they are the ones who deliver the major portion of the company's product. Without this cadre, the company would experience serious consequences.

Management often and loudly states how important this group is, calling them "the face of the company" and "the heart of the program and service." But it's all talk.

The cadre is never consulted about the products and services they deliver. They are the lowest paid and least respected group within the organization. The talk about importance is loud, but hollow.

And the actions of management deliver this message very clearly: "The cadre is not valued."

As members of management, we must not just talk, we must also show!

**When the only tool you have
is a hammer,
every problem begins to look like
a nail.**

Anonymous

Clearly, this motto represents backward thinking. When faced with a task or a challenge, the conditions must determine the appropriate tool. The rule to follow must be this: "Fit the tool to the task, not the other way around."

We see the "only tool" thinking in many business situations, however. Here's an example that will be familiar to anyone who has ever attended a business seminar or convention.

In today's world, as soon as someone is assigned to give a presentation, there is a reflex reaction that results in selecting PowerPoint as the presentation method. Now, this isn't an anti-PowerPoint comment, but, as good as it is, it isn't necessarily the best technique for every situation!

A photograph or a flip chart might be a better device for presenting certain specific information, but too many people default to this computer-driven technique. Years ago most business presenters used 35 mm slides, and it was easy to identify program speakers at a meeting or a conference by looking for the people who were carrying carousel trays. That was once the medium of choice, but now it has been replaced by "high-tech" tools.

When President John F. Kennedy challenged NASA to land a man on the moon, a wide array of new tools was developed to accomplish the task. And it worked!

An observer at the time commented, "If NASA hadn't concentrated on developing new tools and techniques, but used only existing familiar tools . . . they would have put wings on a locomotive." What a disaster that would have been!

Ask yourself this question: "Is this the best tool, or just the most comfortable?"

**The beginning
is the most important part
of the work.**

Plato

I saved this motto for last for two reasons. First, something had to be at the end; but second, this is the last motto I completed.

It took quite a while to get to the end, but I made it.

When I started the book I had only an idea, a pen, and a lot of paper. Obviously, without the pen and paper, the idea would have gone nowhere. Likewise, without the idea, the pen and paper would still be in my desk drawer.

(An editorial note: Yes, I do write the first draft using pen and paper because my typing skills won't allow me to work directly on the computer—but I'm working on that deficiency in my job skills!)

After I wrote the first sentence, the second one was easier, then the third, the fourth, and so on.

Without that first sentence, however, nothing else would have happened.

So whatever it is you want to accomplish in business, start now.

Take a course, ask for an interview, learn a new skill, observe colleagues, find a mentor, take chances, make plans.

Then begin.

Remember: The beginning is the most important part!

A Final Note

I would welcome hearing from you about your experiences
and your mottoes.

I'm sure we can identify more mottoes,
and if we share them,
they may be valuable for all of us in our careers.

All the best.

Throughout the book I've mentioned consulting, coaching, and
teaching.
If you're interested in learning more about my background,
please feel free to visit
my Web site at:
www:jrparkinson.com

or contact me at:
jrp@jrparkinson.com